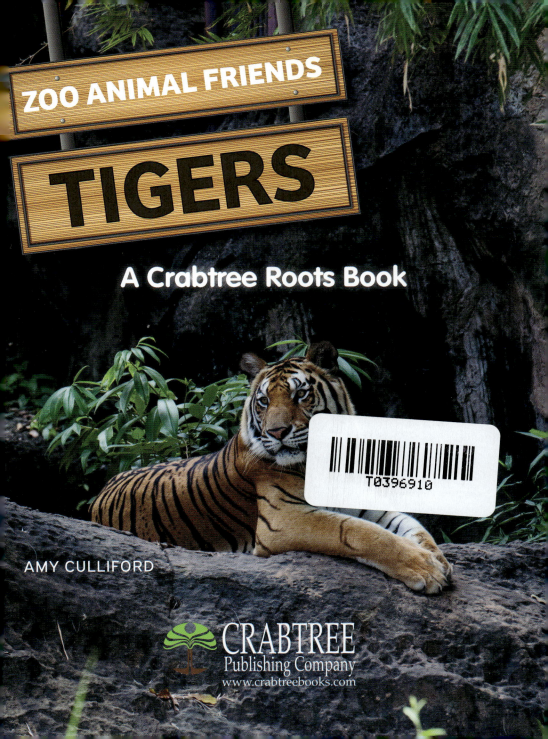

ZOO ANIMAL FRIENDS

TIGERS

A Crabtree Roots Book

AMY CULLIFORD

CRABTREE
Publishing Company
www.crabtreebooks.com

School-to-Home Support for Caregivers and Teachers

This book helps children grow by letting them practice reading. Here are a few guiding questions to help the reader with building his or her comprehension skills. Possible answers appear here in red.

Before Reading:

• What do I think this book is about?
- *I think this book Is about tigers living in a zoo.*
- *I think this book is about tigers and their cubs.*

• What do I want to learn about this topic?
- *I want to learn more about the habitat that tigers live in.*
- *I want to learn how fast a tiger can run.*

During Reading:

• I wonder why...
- *I wonder why tigers have stripes.*
- *I wonder why tigers live in a zoo.*

• What have I learned so far?
- *I have learned that most tigers are orange, black, and white.*
- *I have learned that tigers can be big or small.*

After Reading:

• What details did I learn about this topic?
- *I have learned that tigers have claws.*
- *I have learned that some tigers like water.*

• Read the book again and look for the vocabulary words.
- *I see the word **orange** on page 6 and the word **claws** on page 9. The other vocabulary words are found on page 14.*

This is a **tiger**.

Tigers can be big or little.

Many tigers are **orange**, black, and white.

All tigers have **claws**.

Some tigers like water.

All tigers say, *roar*!

13

Word List

Sight Words

a	can	say
all	have	some
and	is	this
are	like	water
be	little	white
big	many	
black	or	

Words to Know

claws

orange

tiger

29 Words

This is a **tiger**.

Tigers can be big or little.

Many tigers are **orange**, black, and white.

All tigers have **claws**.

Some tigers like water.

All tigers say, *roar*!

Written by: Amy Culliford
Designed by: Rhea Wallace
Series Development : James Earley
Proofreader: Petrice Custance
Educational Consultant: Marie Lemke M.Ed.

Photographs:
Shutterstock: Anna Kaewkhammul: cover; aiddawn: p. 1; Rudi Ernst: p. 3; Cynthia Kidwell: p. 5; Breakingthewalls: p. 7; Suntisook.D: p. 8; hxdbzxy: p. 10-11; Setta Sornnoi: p. 13

Library and Archives Canada Cataloguing in Publication

CIP available at Library and Archives Canada

Library of Congress Cataloging-in-Publication Data

CIP available at Library of Congress

Crabtree Publishing Company

www.crabtreebooks.com   1-800-387-7650

Copyright © 2023 **CRABTREE PUBLISHING COMPANY**   Printed in the U.S.A./072022/CG20220201

All rights reserved. No part of this publication may be reproduced, stored in a retrieval system or be transmitted in any form or by any means, electronic, mechanical, photocopying, recording, or otherwise, without the prior written permission of Crabtree Publishing Company. In Canada: We acknowledge the financial support of the Government of Canada through the Canada Book Fund for our publishing activities.

Published in the United States
Crabtree Publishing
347 Fifth Avenue, Suite 1402-145
New York, NY, 10016

Published in Canada
Crabtree Publishing
616 Welland Ave.
St. Catharines, ON, L2M 5V6